Ketogenic Breakfast

· COOKBOOK ·

Easy, Flavorful and Original Low Carb Recipes
to Lose Belly Fat and Kickstart Your Day!

MARY J. GREEN

Table of Contents

Introduction

The ketogenic diet provides the body with premium fuel in the form of fats that make you fitter and younger with the energy of a twenty-year-old, and the best part, it lasts longer than carb fuel.

By following the ketogenic diet, you can lose all the unwanted weight without ever stepping foot in a gym, without any meal portion control or counting calories.

The ketogenic diet has proven to work for people with all types of background and health issues like having blood sugar issues, obesity, post-pregnancy, people having food addictions, suffering from emotional eating, etc.

Adaptation to ketosis can be tough, and you will need time to adjust to the changes. It is normal, and everyone faces troubles in adapting to any new dietary plan.

However, here are some steps to help you in transiting into the ketogenic diet plan perfectly. Just remember that it does require time, and you will have to give yourself a little space to adjust to the restrictions. It won't happen overnight, so don't be disheartened and stay motivated!

The most basic mistake that many keto dieters make is that they don't gain enough knowledge before starting the diet. Therefore, the most important step is to learn the small differences that make a huge difference.

Understand what keto-friendly foods are, and what foods are not meant for ketosis at all. For example, a lot of apple does not eat an apple because it has many carbs.

However, if you have a medium or a small-sized apple, then you are good to have it. As long as it remains within your carb limit, it is keto-friendly. You can also eat an apple a day (depending on the size), but you need to remember ketosis's essence and take your carbs from energetic sources like protein and healthy fats.

Once you can understand the difference between non-keto and keto-friendly foods, you will notice that ketosis is not that tough after all.

The best way to transit in ketosis is to keep track of your carbs. This might seem annoying at first, but you will gradually see how helpful it is, and you will eventually understand the importance of calculating the net carbs per day. It is extremely crucial, and usually, people overlook this issue quite easily. However, if you want to settle into ketosis perfectly, it is best to keep track of your net carbs.

Mindful eating is a very important step towards transition into ketosis. Your caloric intake has a huge impact on your weight loss. The more calories you take, the harder it gets to lose the stubborn, stored fat.

A keto calculator can be extremely helpful in this matter, though. You can calculate your caloric intake on the go and limit your food intake accordingly. Also, before you pick something to eat, you can instantly calculate the calories you will take.

This is known as mindful eating, knowing what you are eating and how it will affect you. Ketosis is all about gaining knowledge and getting into the habit of mindful eating.

Once you know what you are eating and how much it has to offer to you, you will gradually see major changes in your overall diet routine. You will also find yourself adjusting to ketosis much easier.

Smoothies Recipes

1. Latte Breakfast Smoothie

Prep Time:	Cooking Time:	Servings:
10 min	0 min	2

Ingredients:

- 1 scoop unflavored collagen powder
- 1 tbsp. MCT oil
- 1 tbsp. chia seeds
- 1-2 tbsp. swerve
- ½ tsp. ground cinnamon
- 12 oz. cold brewed coffee
- 1 cup unsweetened almond milk.

Direction:

In blender, add all the ingredients and pulse until smooth.

Transfer into 2 serving glasses and serve immediately.

Nutrition:

Calories 144 kcal | Carbs: 4g | Protein: 15.2g.

2. Velvety Chocolate Smoothie

Prep Time:	Cooking Time:	Servings:
10 min	0 min	2

Ingredients:

- ¼ cup cacao powder
- ¼ cup almond butter
- 1 tbsp. almonds
- 5-6 drops liquid stevia
- 1 cup unsweetened almond milk
- ½ cup unsweetened coconut milk
- ¼ cup ice cubes.

Direction:

Using a high-speed blender, add all the ingredients and pulse until smooth.

Transfer into 2 serving glasses and serve immediately.

Nutrition:

Calories 110 kcal | Carbs: 7.5g | Protein: 3.8g.

3. Golden Chai Latte Smoothie

Prep Time:	Cooking Time:	Servings:
10 min	0 min	2

Ingredients:

- 2 tbsp. chia seeds
- 1 tbsp. ground turmeric
- 1 tsp. ground cinnamon
- 1 tsp. ground ginger
- ¼ tsp. ground cardamom
- Pinch of ground black pepper

- 2 tbsp. MCT oil
- 2 tsp. stevia powder
- 1¾ cup. unsweetened almond milk
- ¼ cup ice cubes.

Direction:

With a high-speed blender, add all the ingredients and pulse until smooth.

Transfer into 2 serving glasses and serve immediately.

Nutrition:

Calories 178 kcal | Carbs: 8.5g | Protein: 2.7g.

4. Creamy Textured Smoothie

Prep Time:	Cooking Time:	Servings:
10 min	0 min	2

Ingredients:

- ½ cup avocado
- 3 tbsp. monk fruit sweetener
- 2 tbsp. natural creamy peanut butter
- 2 tbsp. cacao powder
- 1½ cup unsweetened almond milk
- ½ cup ice, crushed.

Direction:

Process all the ingredients until smooth.

Transfer into 2 serving glasses and serve immediately.

Nutrition:

Calories 222 kcal | Carbs: 10g | Protein: 5.9g.

5. Red Festive Smoothie

Prep Time:	Cooking Time:	Servings:
10 min	0 min	2

Ingredients:

- ¾ cup raw red beets, chopped
- 4 frozen strawberries
- 2-3 drops liquid stevia
- 1½ cup unsweetened almond milk
- ½ cup ice cubes.

Direction:

At high-speed blender, mix all the ingredients and pulse until smooth.

Fill into 2 serving glasses and serve immediately.

Nutrition:

Calories 66 kcal | Carbs: 9g | Protein: 2g.

6. Pretty Pink Smoothie

Prep Time:	Cooking Time:	Servings:
10 min	0 min	2

Ingredients:

- ½ cup fresh strawberries, hulled
- 8-10 fresh basil leaves
- 3-4 drops liquid stevia
- ½ cup plain Greek yogurt
- 1 cup unsweetened almond milk
- ¼ cup ice cubes.

Direction:

In a high-speed blender, incorporate all the ingredients and pulse until smooth.

Pour into 2 serving glasses and serve.

Nutrition:

Calories 73 kcal | Carbs: 8g | Protein: 4.3g.

7. Strawberry Smoothies

Prep Time:	Cooking Time:	Servings:
9 min	0 min	2

Ingredient

- 8 almonds
- 1½ scoops low-carb protein powder
- 2 large strawberries
- 16 oz. unsweetened almond milk
- 6 cubes of ice.

Direction:

Add all of the fixings in your blender.

Wait for the ice to break apart.

Serve in two 10-oz. chilled glasses.

Nutrition

Calories 157 kcal | Protein: 18.9g | Fats: 6.6g.

8. Strawberry & Rhubarb Pie Smoothie

Prep Time:	Cooking Time:	Servings:
12 min	0 min	1

Ingredient

- 2 tbsp. almond butter (or 1 oz. almonds)
- 1.8 oz. medium rhubarb stalks (1-2 stalks)
- 2-4 medium strawberries (or 1.4 oz.)
- 1 large organic/free-range egg
- 2 tbsp. coconut milk - full-fat cream
- ½ cup unsweetened almond milk

- 1 vanilla bean (or ½ tsp. pure vanilla bean extract)
- ½ tsp. ginger root powder (or 1 tsp. freshly grated ginger root)
- 3-6 drops liquid stevia extract – vanilla or clear.

Direction:

Combine each of the ingredients into a blender.

Pulse and enjoy when smooth.

Nutrition

Calories 392 kcal | Protein: 14.2g | Fats: 31.8g.

9. Avocado Smoothie

Prep Time:	Cooking Time:	Servings:
5 min	0 min	1

Ingredient

- 1 avocado
- 6 ice cubes
- 6 drops EZ-Sweetz sweetener
- 3 oz. unsweetened almond milk
- 3 oz. coconut cream.

Direction:

Slice the avocado lengthwise. Remove the seeds and the skin.

Toss the avocado with the rest of the fixings into the blender.

Toss in the ice cubes and blend until the smoothie is creamy smooth.

Nutrition

Calories 587 kcal | Protein: 6g | Fats: 58g.

10 Avocado Mint Green Smoothie

Prep Time:	Cooking Time:	Servings:
11 min	0 min	1

Ingredient:

- 3-4 oz. avocado
- 3 sprigs cilantro
- 5-6 large mint leaves
- ¼ tsp. vanilla extract
- 1 squeeze lime juice
- Sweetener of your choice (as desired)
- ⅛ cup full-fat coconut milk
- ½ cup unsweetened almond milk
- 1½ cup crushed ice.

Direction:

Portion each of the ingredients into the blender.

Puree it using the low-speed setting.

Toss in the ice and mix. Serve in a cold mug.

Nutrition

Calories 221 kcal | Fats: 23g | Protein: 1g.

11. Vanilla Fat-Burning Smoothie

Prep Time:	Cooking Time:	Servings:
7 min	0 min	1

Ingredient:

- ½ cup mascarpone full-fat cheese
- 2 large egg yolks
- ¼ cup water
- 1 tbsp. coconut oil
- 4 ice cubes
- 3 drops liquid stevia extract
- ½ tsp. vanilla extract.

Optional Topping:

- Whipped cream

Direction:

Combine all of the fixings in a blender. Blend until smooth.

Add the whipped cream for a special treat but add the carbs if any.

Nutrition

Calories 651 kcal | Fats: 64g | Protein: 12g.

12. Delightful Chocolate Smoothie

Prep Time:	Cooking Time:	Servings:
6 min	0 min	1

Ingredient:

- 2 large eggs
- 1 tbsp. extra-virgin coconut oil
- 1-2 tbsp. coconut butter
- ¼ cup heavy whipping cream
- 1-2 tbsp. chia seeds
- ½ tsp. cinnamon
- 3-5 drops liquid stevia extract
- ½ cup plain or chocolate whey protein
- 1 tbsp. unsweetened cacao powder
- ¼ cup water
- ½ tsp. vanilla extract
- ½ cup ice.

Direction:

Beat eggs with the rest of fixings into a blender. Pulse until frothy. Add to a chilled glass and enjoy.

Nutrition:

Calories 571 kcal | Protein: 34.5g | Carbs: 23.2g | Fats: 46g.

13. Banana & Berry Smoothie

Prep Time:	Cooking Time:	Servings:
45 min	0 min	2

Ingredient:

- ¼ cup fresh or de-frozen strawberries or blueberries
- 1 ripe banana, sliced and frozen
- 2 cups unsweetened coconut milk
- ½ tsp. vanilla extract
- 6-8 drops liquid stevia extract
- 2 tbsp. MCT oil

- 3 tbsp. golden flaxseed meal
- ½ tbsp. chia seeds
- ¼ tsp. xanthan gum.

Direction:

In a high-speed blender, add all the ingredients except banana and stir, until well combined.

Set aside for at least 30 minutes so that the seeds and flax absorb some of the liquid.

Add in frozen banana slices just before blending. Pulse for few minutes until smooth.

Serve immediately.

Nutrition

Calories 270 kcal | Fats: 23.3g | Carbs: 3.4g | Protein: 3.1g.

14. Blueberry & Almond Smoothie

Prep Time:	Cooking Time:	Servings:
13 min	0 min	2

Ingredient:

- 16 oz. unsweetened almond milk
- 4 oz. heavy cream
- Stevia, to taste
- 1 scoop whey vanilla isolate powder
- ¼ cup frozen or fresh blueberries.

Direction:

Throw all of the fixings into a blender.

Mix until smooth.

Serve it up in a couple of chilled glasses.

Nutrition

Calories 297 kcal | Protein: 14.8g | Carbs: 6.5g | Fats: 24g.

15. Strawberry Yogurt Smoothie

Prep Time:	Cooking Time:	Servings:
16 min	0 min	2

Ingredient:

- 10 strawberries
- ½ cup plain low-fat Greek yogurt
- ½ tsp. vanilla extract
- 1 cup unsweetened coconut milk
- 6 drops liquid stevia extract.

Direction:

In a high-speed blender cup, combine all the ingredients.

Process for about 30 seconds, until creamy and smooth.

Divide between two chilled mugs.

Serve and enjoy!

Nutrition:

Calories 96 kcal | Protein: 3.8g | Carbs: 1.4g | Fats: 5.2g.

16. Chocolate Smoothie

Prep Time:	Cooking Time:	Servings:
9 min	0 min	1

Ingredient:

- ¼ cup unsweetened coconut milk
- ½ ripened avocado
- 1 tsp. cinnamon powder (optional)
- 2 tsp. unsweetened cacao powder
- ¼ tsp. vanilla extract
- 3 drops liquid stevia extract.
- 1 tsp. coconut oil

Direction:

Blend all of the above ingredients for 1-2 minutes until smooth.

Pour into a cup and serve.

Nutrition:

Calories 302 kcal | Protein: 8g | Carbs: 2.1g | Fats: 29.8g.

17. Cinnamon Pear Oatmeal Breakfast Smoothie

Prep Time:	Cooking Time:	Servings:
11 min	0 min	1

Ingredient

- 1 ripe pear, shredded
- 2 tbsp. low-carb protein powder
- 1 tsp. gluten free rolled oats
- 1 cup unsweetened almond milk
- ¼ tsp. vanilla extract
- 3 drops liquid stevia extract
- ½ tsp. cinnamon.

Direction:

In a high-speed blender, combine all the ingredients and stir well.

Set aside for at least 30 minutes so that the oats absorb some of the liquid.

Process for few minutes until smooth.

Serve and enjoy!

Nutrition:

Calories 233 kcal | Protein: 22g | Fats: 1.6g | Carbs: 19.5g.

18. Cucumber Spinach Smoothies

Prep Time:	Cooking Time:	Servings:
7 min	0 min	2

Ingredient

- 6 ice cubes
- Your choice of sweetener, to taste
- ¾ cup coconut milk
- 2 tbsp. MCT oil
- 2½ oz. cucumber
- 2 handfuls of spinach

- 1 cup coconut milk
- ¼ tsp. xanthan gum.

Direction:

Cream the coconut milk: This is a simple process. Chill coconut milk overnight. The next morning, open then scoop out the coconut milk that has solidified. Don't shake the can before opening. Discard the liquids.

Add all of the ingredients, save the ice cubes, to the blender and blend using the low speed until pureed.

Thin with water as needed.

Stir in the ice cubes and blend until the smoothie reaches your desired consistency.

Nutrition:

Calories 330 kcal | Protein: 10g | Fats: 32g.

19. Breakfast Smoothie Bowl

Prep Time:	Cooking Time:	Servings:
10 min	0 min	1

Ingredients:

- 1 medium avocado
- ⅓ cup frozen cauliflower rice
- ⅔ cup fresh or frozen raspberries
- 1 scoop low-carb protein powder
- ½ tsp. vanilla extract
- 1 tsp. Stevia

- 1 tsp. beet powder
- ¼ cup unsweetened almond milk.

Directions:

In a high-speed blender, add all the ingredients and pulse until smooth.

Transfer into 2 bowls.

Serve with your favorite topping.

Nutrition:

Calories 126 kcal| Fat 7.2g | Carbs: 9g | Protein: 13.8g.

20. Creamy Spinach Smoothie Bowl

Prep Time:	Cooking Time:	Servings:
10 min	0 min	1

Ingredient

- ½ cup almond milk
- 1 cup spinach
- 2 tbsp. heavy cream
- 1 scoop low-carb protein powder
- 1 tbsp. coconut oil
- ¼ cup ice cubes.

For Toppings:

- 4 walnuts
- 4 raspberries
- 1 tsp. chia seeds
- 1 tbsp. shredded coconut.

Direction:

Add a cup of spinach to your high-speed blender. Pour in the cream, almond milk, ice, and coconut oil.

Blend for a few seconds until it has an even consistency, and all ingredients are well combined. Empty the goodies into a serving dish.

Arrange your toppings or give them a toss and mix them together. Of course, you can make it pretty and alternate the strips of toppings.

Nutrition

Calories 570 kcal | Protein: 35g | Fats: 35g.

21. Blackberry Cheesecake Smoothie

Prep Time:	Cooking Time:	Servings:
19 min	0 min	1

Ingredient:

- 1 tbsp. extra-virgin coconut oil
- ½ cup fresh/frozen blackberries
- ½ cup water
- ¼ cup coconut milk/heavy whipping cream
- ¼ cup full-fat cream cheese
- ½ tsp. sugar-free vanilla extract
- 3 to 5 drops as desired of Liquid stevia.

Direction:

Arrange all of the fixings in the blender.

Pulse until it's smooth and frothy.

Add a few ice cubes and enjoy it in a chilled glass.

Nutrition:

Calories 515 kcal | Protein: 6g | Fats: 53g.

Sweet Breakfast Recipes

22. Avocado Lime Frozen Yogurt

Prep Time:	Cooking Time:	Servings:
4 h 45 min	0 min	8

Ingredients:

- 2 large ripe avocados
- 1 cup plain Greek yogurt
- ¼ cup unsweetened almond milk
- ¼ cup honey
- ¼ cup lime, juiced
- ⅛ tsp. salt.

For Topping (optional):

- ¼ cup pineapple, diced
- ¼ cup melon, diced
- ¼ cup mango, diced
- ¼ cup passion fruit, diced.

Directions:

Chop avocados into large pieces after slicing them in half, removing pits and peeling off the skin.

In a food processor, combine all the ingredients. Process for about 2-3 minutes, until smooth. If needed, scrape down the sides of the bowl with a spatula.

Put the mixture into a medium freezer-safe container. Freeze for 30 to 45 minutes.

Pure the yogurt mixture into a high-speed blender and process about 2-3 minutes, until creamy.

Return the yogurt mixture into the container and place it back into freezer for another 30-45 minutes.

Repeat the process 2 times more.

After the third mixing, freeze the yogurt mixture for at least 3 hours (or overnight).

Remove the yogurt mixture from freezer few minutes before serving. Let it cool a bit, until softened, then scoop into serving bowls.

Serve immediately topped with fresh diced tropical fruit to your choice, if desired.

Nutrition:

Calories 112 kcal | Protein: 4g | Carbs: 13g | Fat: 8g.

23. Keto Friendly Protein Chia Pudding

Prep Time:	Cooking Time:	Servings:
10 min	1 h	4

Ingredient:

- 3 cups full fat coconut milk (canned)
- 3 tbsp. granulated stevia
- ½ cup fresh or frozen berry mix
- 2 tbsp. low-carb protein powder
- ½ tsp. vanilla extract
- 2 tbsp. coconut butter
- ⅛ tsp. salt
- 8 tbsp. chia seeds.

Toppings (optional)

- Fresh strawberries
- Fresh blueberries
- Fresh raspberries
- Fresh blackberries
- Fresh cherries, pitted
- Coconut flakes
- Almond flakes
- Low carb homemade granola

Direction:

In a high-speed blender, add coconut milk, stevia, berry mix, protein powder, coconut butter and salt. Blend well, until creamy and smooth.

In a large bowl, add chia seeds. Then add in the berry-coconut batter and stir well.

Refrigerate for at least 1 hour (or overnight).

Dish up right before serving and add your toppings of choice.

Nutrition:

Calories 470 kcal | Fat: 43g | Carbs: 5.7g | Protein: 7.1g.

24. Peanut Butter Power Granola

Prep Time:	Cooking Time:	Servings:
10 min	40 min	12

Ingredient:

- 1 cup almond flour
- 1½ cup almonds
- 1½ cup pecans
- ⅓ cup swerve sweetener
- ⅓ cup vanilla whey protein powder
- ⅓ cup peanut butter
- ¼ cup sunflower seeds
- ¼ cup butter
- ¼ cup water.

Direction:

Set oven to 300°F and prep a baking sheet with parchment paper.

Pulse the almonds and pecans in a food processor.

Put them all in a large bowl and add the sunflower seeds, shredded coconut, vanilla, sweetener, and protein powder.

Melt the peanut butter and butter together in the microwave.

Mix the melted butter in the nut mixture and stir it thoroughly until the nuts are well-distributed.

Put in the water to create a lumpy mixture.

Scoop out small amounts of the mixture and place it on the baking sheet.

Bake for 30 minutes. Enjoy!

Nutrition:

Calories 338 kcal | Fat: 30g | Carbs: 9.7g | Protein: 9.6g.

25. Cinnamon and Spice Overnight Oats

Prep Time:	Cooking Time:	Servings:
5 min	1 h	1

Ingredients

- 2.5 oz. rolled oats
- ½ cup milk
- 2.5 oz. yogurt
- 1 tsp. honey
- ½ tsp. vanilla extract
- ⅛ tsp. ground cinnamon
- 0.7 oz. raisins.

Direction

Incorporate all ingredients well.

Chill overnight or at least one hour.

Remove from the fridge or heat it in the microwave immediately or slowly.

Nutrition

Calories 182 kcal | Carbs: 15g | Protein: 26g | Fat: 34g.

26. Nutty Textured Porridge

Prep Time:	Cooking Time:	Servings:
15 min	35 min	5

Ingredients:

- ½ cup pecans
- ½ cup walnuts
- ¼ cup sunflower seeds
- ¼ cup chia seeds
- ¼ cup unsweetened coconut flakes
- 4 cups unsweetened almond milk
- ½ tsp. ground cinnamon
- ¼ tsp. ground ginger
- 1 tsp. stevia powder
- 1 tbsp. butter.

Directions:

In a food processor, place the pecans, walnuts and sunflower seeds and pulse until a crumbly mixture is formed.

In a large pan, add the nuts mixture, chia seeds, coconut flakes, almond milk, spices and stevia powder over medium heat.

Bring to a gentle simmer, stirring frequently.

Select heat to low and simmer for about 20-30 minutes, stirring frequently.

Remove from the heat and serve hot with the topping of butter.

Nutrition:

Calories 269 kcal | Fat: 6.2g | Carbs: 8.6g | Protein: 7g.

27. Berry Hot Cereal

Prep Time:	Cooking Time:	Servings:
8 min	20 min	4

Ingredients

- 2 cups whole rolled oats
- 4 cups of water
- 2 cups low-fat milk
- 2 tbsp. honey
- ½ tsp. salt
- ½ cup almond flakes, toasted

For Topping

- ½ cup fresh raspberries
- ½ cup fresh blueberries

Direction

In a saucepan, boil water at high heat and add the salt.

Stir in the oats and milk, then reduce the heat to low and cover.

Cook according to package instructions, or until the oatmeal reaches the desired consistency, about 20 minutes.

Remove from heat and stir in almonds and honey.

Divide the oatmeal between 4 deep bowls.

Top each bowl with mixed raspberries and blueberries in equal parts and serve.

Nutrition

Calories 210 kcal | Fat: 14.9g | Carbs 11.5g | Protein: 20g.

28. Blueberry Waffles

Prep Time:	Cooking Time:	Servings:
11 min	17 min	9

Ingredient:

- 8 medium eggs
- 5 oz. butter, melted
- 1 tsp. vanilla extract
- 2 tsp. low-carb baking powder
- ⅓ cup coconut flour.

For Topping:

- 3 oz. butter
- 1 oz. fresh blueberries.

Direction:

Heat your waffle iron to medium temperature.

Start by mixing the butter and eggs first until you get a smooth batter.

Put in the remaining ingredients except those that you will be using as topping.

Pour the batter in a waffle iron and cook until golden brown.

In a small bowl, combine butter and blueberries and mix until creamy, using a hand mixer.

Top freshly cooked waffles with blueberry cream and serve.

Nutrition:

Calories 573 kcal| Fat 54g | Carbs: 12.1g | Fiber 4.9g | Protein: 35.7g.

29. Crispy Keto Waffles

Prep Time:	Cooking Time:	Servings:
17 min	18 min	5

Ingredients:

- ½ cup super fine almond flour
- ½ tsp. Stevia
- ¼ tsp. baking soda
- ¼ tsp. low-carb baking powder
- ¼ tsp. ground cinnamon
- ⅛ tsp. cloves, ground
- ⅛ tsp. nutmeg, ground
- A pinch of salt
- 2 tbsp. butter, melted
- 2 large eggs, yolks and whites separated
- 1 tsp. vanilla extract.

Directions:

Preheat the waffle iron.

In a bowl, add the flour, Stevia, baking soda, baking powder, spices and salt and mix until smooth.

In a separate small bowl, combine the butter, egg yolks, and vanilla. Beat well.

In a third small bowl, beat egg whites until soft peaks form.

Add the egg yolks mixture into flour mixture and stir until well combined.

Gently, fold in the beaten egg whites.

Place ¼ of the mixture into your waffle iron and cook for 4 to 5 minutes, until golden brown.

Repeat with the remaining mixture.

Nutrition:

Calories 167 kcal | Carbs: 3.9g | Protein: 5.6g.

30. Protein Waffle

Prep Time:	Cooking Time:	Servings:
5 min	10 min	2

Ingredients:

- 1 egg, lightly beaten
- 1 tbsp. unsweetened almond milk
- 1 scoop low-carb protein powder
- ¼ tsp. gluten-free baking powder
- 1 tbsp. butter, melted
- ¼ tsp. salt.

Directions:

Incorporate all ingredients in a bowl.

Spray waffle maker with cooking spray.

Pour ½ of the batter in waffle maker and cook until golden brown.

Repeat with the remaining batter.

Nutrition

Calories 160 kcal | Fat: 10.7g | Carbs: 2.7g.

31. Almond Flour Waffle

Prep Time:	Cooking Time:	Servings:
5 min	10 min	8

Ingredients:

- 2 cups almond flour
- 8 medium eggs, lightly beaten
- ½ cup heavy cream
- ⅛ tsp. salt.

Directions:

Preheat your waffle maker.

Whisk all ingredients in a mixing bowl.

Spray waffle maker with cooking spray.

Cook ⅛ batter in the waffle maker until golden brown.

Repeat with the remaining batter.

Enjoy!

Nutrition

Calories 249 kcal | Fat: 21g | Carbs: 6g.

32. Banana Waffle

Prep Time:	Cooking Time:	Servings:
10 min	30 min	4

Ingredient:

- 4 eggs, beaten
- 1 ripe banana, mashed
- ¾ cup coconut milk
- ¾ cup almond flour
- 1 pinch salt
- 1 tbsp. ground psyllium husk powder

- ½ tsp. vanilla extract
- 1 tsp. baking powder
- 1 tsp. ground cinnamon
- Butter or coconut oil for frying

For Topping (optional):

- Hazelnut spread
- Banana slices
- Fresh berries

Direction:

Combine all the ingredients in and whisk thoroughly to distribute the dry and wet ingredients evenly.

You should be able to get a pancake-like consistency.

Fry the waffles in a pan or use a waffle maker.

You can serve it with hazelnut spread, banana slices, or fresh berries, to taste.

Enjoy!

Nutrition:

Calories 157 | Fat | 22.3g | Protein: 6g | Carbs 14g.

33. Chocolate Waffle

Prep Time:	Cooking Time:	Servings:
5 min	15 min	2

Ingredients:

- 3 large organic eggs
- ¼ cup Stevia
- ½ cup butter
- ½ cup unsweetened chocolate chips
- ½ tsp. vanilla

For Topping (optional):

- Honey
- Banana
- Fresh strawberries

Directions:

Add chocolate chips and butter in microwave-safe bowl and microwave for 1 minute. Mix well.

In a bowl, whisk eggs with vanilla and Stevia until frothy.

Add butter-chocolate mixture in the egg mixture and stir well.

Preheat the waffle maker.

Spray it with cooking spray.

Pour ¼ batter in the hot waffle maker.

Cook for 6 to 8 minutes or until golden brown.

Repeat with the remaining batter.

Serve chocolate waffles topped with honey, banana or fresh strawberries and enjoy!

Nutrition

Calories 674 kcal | Fat: 70g | Carbs: 11g | Protein 4g.

34. Keto Low Carb Pancakes

Prep Time:	Cooking Time:	Servings:
5 min	15 min	4-6

Ingredients:

- ½ cup almond flour
- 5 medium eggs
- 4 oz. cream cheese, softened
- 1 tsp. lemon zest
- Butter, as needed, for frying

For Topping (optional):

- Butter, to taste
- Fresh berries, to taste

Directions:

In a medium bowl, whisk together almond flour, eggs, cream cheese, and lemon zest until smooth.

In a nonstick skillet over medium-low heat, melt 1 tablespoon butter.

Pour in about 3 tablespoons batter and cook until golden, for about 2 minutes.

Flip and cook 2 minutes more.

Transfer to a plate.

Repeat with remaining batter.

Serve low carb keto pancakes topped with butter and fresh berries.

Enjoy!

Nutrition

Calories 110 kcal | Fat: 3.5g | Carbs: 2g | Protein: 4g.

35. Pumpkin Cinnamon Muffins

Prep Time:	Cooking Time:	Servings:
10 min	15 min	20

Ingredients:

- ½ cup almond butter
- ½ cup pumpkin, pureed
- ½ cup coconut oil
- 1 tbsp. cinnamon
- 2 scoops vanilla protein powder
- 1 tsp. baking powder
- ½ cup almond flour.

Directions:

Preheat your oven to 350°F.

Grease muffin tray with cooking spray and set aside.

In a large bowl, mix together all dry ingredients.

Add wet ingredients into the dry ingredients and mix until well combined.

Pour batter into the prepared muffin tray.

Bake for 15 minutes, until golden.

Muffins are ready if the toothpick inserted into the center of a muffin comes out clean.

Repeat with remaining batter.

Let cool completely before serving.

Nutrition

Calories 81 kcal | Fat: 7.1g | Protein 5.4g | Carbs: 1.5g.

36. Keto Cherry Muffins

Prep Time:	Cooking Time:	Servings:
15 min	40 min	6

Ingredients:

- 2½ cup almond flour
- ⅓ cup stevia
- ½ tsp. baking soda
- 1½ tsp. baking powder
- ½ tsp. salt
- ⅓ cup unsweetened almond milk
- 3 large eggs
- ⅓ cup melted butter
- 1 tsp. pure vanilla extract
- ⅔ cup fresh or frozen cherries, pitted, de-frozen
- ½ lemon zest.

Directions:

Preheat your oven to 350°F.

Line a 12 cups muffin tin with muffin baking paper cups.

In a large bowl, combine almond flour, Stevia, baking powder, baking soda, and salt. Mix well.

Whisk in almond milk, eggs, melted butter, and vanilla until just combined.

Gently fold cherries and lemon zest until evenly distributed.

Scoop equal amounts of batter into each muffin paper cup.

Bake for about 23 minutes, until slightly golden.

Muffins are ready if the toothpick inserted into the center of a muffin comes out clean.

Let cool completely.

Serve and enjoy!

Nutrition:

Calories 489 | Fat 11g | Carbs: 9.5g | Protein: 10.8g.

37. Low Carb Avocado Brownies

Prep Time:	Cooking Time:	Servings:
10 min	25 min	10

Ingredients:

- 1 large avocado, well mashed
- ½ cup almond butter
- 3 tbsp. Stevia
- 2 tbsp. cocoa powder
- 1 tbsp. olive oil
- 1 tsp. vanilla extract
- ½ cup dark chocolate baking chips
- ¼ cup chopped pecans (optional).

Directions:

Preheat the oven to 350°F. Greased well 8x8 inch baking pan.

In a medium mixing bowl, combine mashed avocado and almond butter, beat on high until the mixture is smooth, for about 2 minutes.

Mix in stevia and cocoa powder. Blend until ingredients are well combined.

Add in olive oil and vanilla extract. Stir well until mixture is smooth.

Put in baking chips and chopped pecans.

Spread the mixture into a prepared baking pan and bake the brownies for 20 to 25 minutes.

Let cool completely before serving. Enjoy!

Nutrition:

Calories 681 kcal | Protein: 8.7g | Fat: 21.8g | Carbs: 7g.

38. Chocolate Mug Cake

Prep Time:	Cooking Time:	Servings:
2 min	2 min	2

Ingredients:

- 2 tbsp. almond four
- 1 tbsp. cocoa powder
- 1 tbsp. Stevia
- ½ tsp. baking powder
- ¼ tsp. vanilla extract
- 1 egg

- 1 pinch sea salt
- 1½ tbsp. melted coconut oil or butter
- ½ oz. sugar-free dark chocolate
- ½ tsp. coconut oil or butter for greasing the mugs.

Directions:

In a small bowl, put all the dry ingredients and mix well.

Stir in egg and melted coconut oil or butter. Mix until smooth.

Add coarsely chopped chocolate and pour into two well-greased coffee mugs.

Microwave for 90 seconds. Remove and let cool.

Serve with a dollop of whipped coconut cream.

Nutrition:

Calories 230 kcal | Protein: 6g | Fat: 21g | Carbs: 4.3g.

39. Lemon Mug Cake

Prep Time:	Cooking Time:	Servings:
5 min	2 min	1

Ingredients:

- 3 tbsp. almond flour
- ½ tsp. low-carb baking powder
- 1 tbsp. unsalted butter, melted
- 1 organic egg
- 2 tbsp. stevia
- ½ tsp. vanilla extract
- 1 tsp. lemon juice
- ½ tbsp. heavy whipping cream

Directions:

In a microwaveable cup, add all the ingredients and whisk until smooth and well combined.

Microwave for 90 seconds. Remove and let cool.

Top with a dollop of heavy whipping cream and serve.

Nutrition:

Calories 227 kcal | Protein: 8.5g | Fat: 22g | Carbs: 3g.

Savory Breakfast Recipes

40. Tomato Frittata

Ingredients:

- 6 eggs
- ⅔ cup cherry tomatoes, halved
- ⅔ cup feta cheese, crumbled
- 1 small onion, sliced
- 1 tbsp. chives, chopped
- 1½ tbsp. basil, chopped

- 1 tbsp. butter
- Fresh ground black pepper, to taste
- Sea salt, to taste.

Directions:

Preheat the oven to 400°F.

Heat up butter in a pan over medium heat.

Sauté onion to the pan.

In a small bowl, whisk eggs with chives, basil, pepper, and salt.

Once onions are done, add egg mixture and cook for 2-3 minutes.

Top with cheese and cherry tomatoes.

Place in oven and cook for 5-7 minutes.

Nutrition

Calories 394 kcal | Fat: 29g | Carbs: 8g | Protein: 24g.

41. Mushroom Omelet

Prep Time:	Cooking Time:	Servings:
10 min	5 min	1

Ingredient:

- 3 medium eggs
- 1 oz. cheese, shredded
- 1 oz. butter used for frying
- ¼ yellow onion, chopped
- 4 large mushrooms, sliced
- Fresh ground black pepper, to taste
- Salt, to taste.

Direction:

Scourge eggs in a bowl. Add some salt and pepper to taste.

Cook butter in a pan using low heat. Put in the mushroom and onion, cooking the two until you get that amazing smell.

Pour the egg mix into the pan and allow it to cook on medium heat.

Allow the bottom part to cook before sprinkling the cheese on top of the still-raw portion of the egg.

Carefully pry the edges of the omelet and fold it in half. Allow it to cook for a few more seconds before removing the pan from the heat and sliding it directly onto your plate.

Nutrition:

Calories 520 kcal | Fat: 27g | Carbs: 5g | Protein: 26g.

42. Keto Omelet

Prep Time:	Cooking Time:	Servings:
10 min	5 min	4

Ingredients:

- 4 large eggs
- 2 oz. cheddar cheese, shredded
- 8 olives, pitted
- 2 tbsp. butter
- 2 tbsp. olive oil
- 1 tsp. herb de Provence

- ½ tsp. salt
- Fresh ground black pepper, to taste
- Your favorite vegetables (optional).

Directions:

Whisk eggs in a bowl with salt, olives, herb de Provence, and olive oil.

Melt butter in a large pan over medium heat.

Pour egg mixture into the hot pan and spread evenly.

Cover and cook for 3 minutes or until omelet lightly golden brown.

Flip omelet to the other side and cook for 2 minutes more.

Serve and enjoy.

Nutrition

Calories 251 kcal | Fat: 22g | Carbs 1.1g | Protein: 16g.

43. Mexican Frittata

Prep Time:	Cooking Time:	Servings:
10 min	20 min	6

Ingredients:

- 8 eggs, scrambled
- ½ cup salsa
- 2 tsp. taco seasoning, homemade
- ½ lb. ground beef
- ½ cup cheddar cheese, grated
- 2 tbsp. green onion, chopped
- ⅓ lb. tomatoes, sliced
- 1 small green pepper, chopped
- 1 tbsp. olive oil
- Fresh ground black pepper, to taste
- Sea salt, to taste.

Directions:

Preheat the oven to 375°F.

Cook oil in a pan over medium heat.

Fry beef until browned.

Add salsa and taco seasoning and stir to coat.

Remove meat from the pan and place on a plate.

Add green pepper to the pan and cook for a few minutes.

Return meat to the pan along with green onion and tomato.

Add scrambled eggs on top then sprinkle with grated cheese.

Bake for 20-25 minutes.

Nutrition

Calories 227 kcal | Fat: 13.8g | Carbs: 4g | Protein: 12.6g.

44. Spinach & Swiss Cheese Omelet

Prep Time:	Cooking Time:	Servings:
11 min	8 min	2

Ingredients

- 1 tsp. olive oil
- 6 large egg whites, beaten
- 1 cup fresh baby spinach leaves
- 2 (1-ounce) slices reduced-fat Swiss cheese
- Fresh ground black pepper, to taste
- Sea salt, to taste.

Direction

In a small skillet, cook olive oil over medium-high heat.

Sauté spinach, salt, and pepper for 3 minutes, stirring often.

Lay out spinach evenly at the bottom, and transfer egg whites over the top, leaning the pan to coat the spinach thoroughly.

Cook for 4 minutes, rarely pulling the edges of the eggs toward the center as you tilt the skillet to allow uncooked egg to spread to the sides of the pan.

Turnover eggs.

Put the Swiss cheese cuts on one half of the omelet, and then turn it over to form a half-moon. Cook for 1 minute.

Nutrition

Calories 234 kcal | Fat: 8g | Carbs: 12g | Protein: 18g.

45. Easy Halloumi Cheese Chaffle

Prep Time:	Cooking Time:	Servings:
5 min	10 min	2

Ingredients:

- 3 oz. Halloumi cheese

Directions:

Cut Halloumi cheese into ½-inch thick slices.

Place one cheese slice in the waffle maker and cook for 5-6 minutes or until golden brown.

Repeat with the remaining cheese slice.

Nutrition

Calories 155 kcal | Fat: 12.7g | Carbs: 1.1g | Protein: 11g.

46. Tasty Omelet Chaffle

Prep Time:	Cooking Time:	Servings:
5 min	3 min	1

Ingredients:

- 2 eggs, lightly beaten
- 1 tbsp. bell pepper, chopped
- 1 tbsp. ham, chopped
- 2 tbsp. cheddar cheese, shredded
- 2 tbsp. almond milk
- Pepper
- Salt.

Directions:

Preheat the waffle maker.

In a bowl, whisk eggs. Add remaining ingredients and stir well.

Coat waffle maker with cooking spray.

Fill in batter in the hot waffle maker and cook for 2-3 minutes or until set. Serve and enjoy.

Nutrition

Calories 304 kcal | Fat: 22g | Carbs: 12g | Protein: 20.4g.

47. Sausage & Cheese Chaffle

Prep Time:	Cooking Time:	Servings:
5 min	15 min	6

Ingredients:

- ½ lb. Italian sausage
- ½ cup cheddar cheese, shredded
- ½ cup almond flour
- 1 egg, lightly beaten
- 2 tbsp. parmesan cheese, grated.

Directions:

Preheat waffle maker.

Combine all ingredients.

Spray waffle maker with cooking spray.

Pour 3 tablespoons of mix in the waffle maker and cook.

Repeat with the rest of the batter.

Nutrition

Calories 234 kcal | Fat: 19.4g | Carbs: 2.6g | Protein: 10.6g.

48. Zingy Scramble

Prep Time:	Cooking Time:	Servings:
13 min	9 min	3

Ingredients:

- 2 tbsp. unsalted butter
- 1 tomato
- 1 scallion
- 2 pickled jalapeños
- 6 organic eggs
- 3 oz. Colby jack cheese
- Salt and black pepper, to taste.

Directions:

In a big frying pan, cook butter over medium-high heat and cook the tomato, scallion and jalapeños for about 3-4 minutes, stirring frequently. Add the eggs and cook for about 2 minutes, stirring continuously.

Stir in the cheese, salt and black pepper and remove from the heat.

Nutrition:

Calories 235 | Fat: 12.7g | Carbs: 2.7g | Protein: 13.2g.

49. Keto Muffins

Prep Time:	Cooking Time:	Servings:
15 min	25 min	6

Ingredients:

- Cooking spray, for pan
- 12 eggs
- ½ cup fresh spinach, shredded
- ¼ tsp. garlic powder
- ¾ cup ham, diced and cooked
- 3 tbsp. onion, chopped
- 1 cup cheddar cheese, shredded

- ¼ cup mushrooms, chopped and sautéed
- ¼ cup bell pepper, diced
- Salt, to taste
- Black ground pepper, to taste.

Directions:

Preheat the oven to 350°F.

Coat muffin tray with cooking spray and set aside.

In a large bowl, beat eggs.

Add remaining ingredients to the bowl and mix well together.

Pour egg mixture into the prepared muffin tray.

Bake for 20-25 minutes.

Nutrition

Calories 243 kcal | Fat: 17g | Carbs: 2.8g | Protein: 16.9g.

50. Mini Crustless Quiches

Prep Time:	Cooking Time:	Servings:
15 min	30 min	6

Ingredients:

- 1 tsp. olive oil
- 1½ cup fresh mushrooms
- 1 scallion
- 1 tsp. garlic, mince
- 1 tsp. fresh rosemary, minced
- 1 (12.3-oz.) package lite firm silken tofu
- ¼ cup unsweetened almond milk
- 2 tbsp. Parmesan cheese
- 1 tbsp. arrowroot starch
- 1 tsp. butter, softened
- ¼ tsp. ground turmeric.

Direction:

Set oven at 375°F. Grease a 12 cups muffin tin.

In a nonstick skillet, heat the oil over medium heat and sauté the scallion and garlic for about 1 minute.

Add the mushrooms and sauté for about 5-7 minutes.

Stir in the rosemary and black pepper and remove from the heat. Set aside to cool slightly.

In a food processor, add the tofu and remaining ingredients and pulse until smooth.

Transfer the tofu mixture into a large bowl.

Fold in the mushroom mixture. Place the mixture into the prepared muffin cups evenly. Bake for about 20-22 minutes.

Remove the muffin pan from the oven and place onto a wire rack to cool for about 10 minutes.

Carefully, invert the muffins onto wire rack and serve warm.

Nutrition:

Calories 77 kcal | Fat: 8.7g | Carbs: 5.3g | Protein: 6.9g.

51. Cheese Jalapeno Muffins

Prep Time:	Cooking Time:	Servings:
10 min	20 min	12

Ingredients:

- Cooking spray, for pan
- 9 eggs
- 6 bacon slices
- ¾ cup heavy cream
- 1½ jalapeno pepper, sliced
- 8.5 oz. cheddar cheese, shredded

- Salt, to taste
- Black ground pepper, to taste.

Directions:

Preheat the oven to 350°F.

Prep muffin tray with cooking spray and add cooked bacon slices to each muffin cup.

In a large bowl, whisk together eggs, cheese, cream, pepper, and salt.

Pour egg mixture into the prepared muffin tray.

Add sliced jalapeno into each muffin cup.

Bake for 15-20 minutes.

Let cool before serving.

Nutrition

Calories 228 kcal | Fat: 18.4g | Carbs: 1g.

52. Anti-Inflammatory Muffins

Prep Time:	Cooking Time:	Servings:
10 min	23 min	6

Ingredients:

- 2 cups almond flour
- ½ cup powdered Swerve
- 3 scoops turmeric tonic
- 1½ tsp. organic baking powder
- 3 organic eggs
- 1 cup mayonnaise
- ½ tsp. organic vanilla extract.

Directions:

Ready the oven to 350°F.

Line a 12 cups muffin tin with paper liners.

In a large bowl, add the flour, Swerve, turmeric tonic and baking powder and mix well.

Add the eggs, mayonnaise and vanilla extract and beat until well combined.

Place the mixture into the prepared muffin cups evenly. Bake for about 20-23 minutes.

Pull out the muffin tin. Position onto the wire rack to cool for 8 minutes.

Carefully invert the muffins onto the wire rack to cool completely before serving.

Nutrition:

Calories 489 | Carbs: 9.5g | Protein: 10.8g.

53. Zucchini Muffins

Prep Time:	Cooking Time:	Servings:
15 min	15 min	4

Ingredients:

- 4 organic eggs
- ¼ cup unsalted butter, melted
- ¼ cup water
- ⅓ cup coconut flour
- ½ tsp. organic baking powder
- ¼ tsp. salt
- 1½ cups zucchini, grated

- ½ cup Parmesan cheese, shredded
- 1 tbsp. fresh oregano, minced
- 1 tbsp. fresh thyme, minced
- ¼ cup cheddar cheese, grated.

Direction:

Preheat the oven to 400°F.

Lightly, grease 8 muffin tins.

Add eggs, butter, and water in a mixing bowl and beat until well combined.

Add the flour, baking powder, and salt, and mix well.

Add remaining ingredients except for cheddar and mix until just combined.

Place the mixture into prepared muffin cups evenly.

Bake for approximately 13–15 minutes or until top of muffins become golden-brown.

Remove the muffin tin from oven and situate onto a wire rack for 10 minutes.

Carefully invert the muffins onto a platter and serve warm.

Nutrition:

Calories 287 kcal | Fat: 23g | Carbs: 8.7g | Protein: 13.2g.

54. Cheese & Bacon Mug Cakes

Prep Time:	Cooking Time:	Servings:
10 min	30 min	2

Ingredients:

- ¼ cup flax meal
- 1 egg
- 2 tbsp. heavy cream
- ¼ cup almond flour
- ¼ tsp. baking soda.

Filling:

- 2 tbsp. cream cheese
- 4 slices bacon
- ½ medium avocado, sliced.

Directions:

Mix together the dry muffin ingredients in a bowl. Add egg, and heavy cream, and whisk well with a fork. Season with salt and pepper.

Divide the mixture between two ramekins.

Place in the microwave and cook for 60-90 seconds.

Leave to cool slightly before filling.

In a skillet, over medium heat, cook the bacon slices until crispy. Transfer to paper towels to soak up excess fat; set aside.

Invert the muffins onto a plate and cut in half, crosswise.

To assemble the cakes: spread cream cheese and top with bacon and avocado slices.

Nutrition:

Calories 511 kcal | Fat: 38.2g | Carbs: 12.7g | Protein: 16.4g.

55. Cheese Jalapeno Bread

Prep Time:	Cooking Time:	Servings:
10 min	15 min	4

Ingredients:

- 4 eggs
- ⅓ cup coconut flour
- ¼ cup water
- ¼ cup butter
- ¼ tsp. pepper
- 3 jalapeno chilies, chopped
- ¼ tsp. onion powder
- ½ cup cheddar cheese, grated
- ¼ cup parmesan cheese, grated
- ¼ tsp. baking powder, gluten-free
- ½ tsp. garlic powder
- ½ tsp. salt.

Directions:

Preheat the oven to 400°F.

In a bowl, mix together eggs, pepper, salt, water, and butter.

Add baking powder, garlic powder, onion powder, and coconut flour and mix well.

Add jalapenos, cheddar cheese, and parmesan cheese. Mix well and season with pepper.

Line baking tray with parchment pepper.

Pour batter into a baking tray and spread evenly.

Bake for 15 minutes.

Nutrition

Calories 249 kcal | Fat: 22g | Carbs: 2.7g.

56. Chicken Quesadillas

Prep Time:	Cooking Time:	Servings:
10 min	15 min	2

Ingredients:

- 1½ cups Mozzarella cheese, shredded
- 1½ cups Cheddar cheese, shredded
- 1 cup chicken, cooked and shredded
- 1 bell pepper, sliced
- ¼ cup tomato, diced
- ⅛ cup green onion
- 1 tbsp. extra-virgin olive oil

Directions:

Preheat the oven to 400°F.

Use parchment paper to cover a pizza pan.

Combine your cheeses and bake the cheese shell for about 5 minutes.

Put the chicken on one half of the cheese shell.

Add peppers, tomatoes, green onion and fold your shell in half over the fillings.

Return your folded cheese shell to the oven again for 4-5 minutes.

Nutrition:

Calories 244 kcal | Fat: 40.5g | Carbs: 6.1g. | Protein: 52.7g.

57. Swiss Cheese Crunchy Nachos

Prep Time:	Cooking Time:	Servings:
5 min	20 min	2

Ingredient:

- ½ cup Swiss cheese, shredded
- ½ cup Cheddar cheese, shredded
- ⅛ cup cooked bacon pieces.

Direction:

Set oven to 300°F and prepare the baking sheet by lining it with parchment paper.

Start by spreading the Swiss cheese on the parchment. Sprinkle it with bacon and then top it off again with the Cheddar cheese.

Bake until the cheese has melted. This should take around 10 minutes or less.

Allow the cheese to cool before cutting them into triangle strips.

Grab another baking sheet and place the triangle cheese strips on top. Broil them for 2 to 3 minutes so they'll get chunky.

Nutrition:

Calories 280 kcal | Fat: 21.8g | Carbs: 4.4g | Protein: 18.6g.

58. Cheese Cauliflower Hash Browns

Prep Time:	Cooking Time:	Servings:
10 min	15 min	6

Ingredients:

- 3 cups cauliflower, grated
- ¾ cup cheddar cheese, shredded
- 1 egg, lightly beaten
- ½ tsp. garlic powder
- ½ tsp. cayenne pepper
- ¼ tsp. pepper
- ½ tsp. salt.

Directions:

Blend all ingredients into the bowl.

Grease baking tray with cooking spray and set aside.

Make six hash browns from cauliflower mixture and place on a prepared baking tray.

Bake at 400°F for 15 minutes.

Nutrition

Calories 81 kcal | Fat: 5g | Carbs: 3.4g.

59. Avocado Taco

Prep Time:	Cooking Time:	Servings:
10 min	15 min	6

Ingredients:

- 1-pound ground beef
- 3 avocados, halved
- 1 tbsp. Chili powder
- ½ tsp. salt
- ¾ tsp. cumin
- ½ tsp. oregano, dried
- ¼ tsp. garlic powder
- ¼ tsp. onion powder
- 8 tbsp. tomato sauce
- 1 cup Cheddar cheese, shredded
- ¼ cup cherry tomatoes, sliced
- ¼ cup lettuce, shredded
- ½ cup sour cream.

Directions:

Pit halved avocados. Set aside.

Place the ground beef into a saucepan. Cook at medium heat until it is browned.

Add the seasoning and tomato sauce. Stir well and cook for about 4 minutes.

Load each avocado half with the beef.

Top with shredded cheese and lettuce, tomato slices, and sour cream.

Nutrition:

Calories 278 kcal | Fat: 22g | Carbs: 14g | Protein: 18g.

60. Spinach & Feta Breakfast Wraps

Prep Time:	Cooking Time:	Servings:
13 min	6 min	2

Ingredients

- 1 tsp. olive oil
- ½ cup fresh baby spinach leaves
- 1 tbsp. fresh basil
- 4 egg whites, beaten
- ½ tsp. salt
- ¼ tsp. freshly ground black pepper

- ¼ cup crumbled low-fat feta cheese
- 2 (8-inch) whole-wheat tortillas.

Direction

Heat up olive oil on medium heat.

Sauté spinach and basil to the pan for about 2 minutes.

Add the egg whites to the pan, season with the salt and pepper, and sauté, often stirring, for about 2 minutes more, or until the egg whites are firm.

Remove from the heat and sprinkle with the feta cheese.

Warm up tortillas in the microwave for 20 to 30 seconds.

Divide the eggs between the tortillas and wrap up burrito-style.

Nutrition

Calories 224 kcal | Fat: 10.4g | Carbs: 4.5g | Protein: 10.6g.

61. Spicy Breakfast Sausage

Prep Time:	Cooking Time:	Servings:
3 min	12 min	4

Ingredients:

- 4 chicken sausages, sliced
- 1 chili pepper, minced
- 1 cup shallots, diced
- ¼ cup dry white wine
- 2 tsp. lard, room temperature
- 2 tsp. garlic, minced

- Spanish peppers, deveined and chopped
- 2 tbsp. fresh coriander, minced
- 2 tsp. balsamic vinegar
- 1 cup pureed tomatoes.

Directions:

In a frying pan, warm the lard over a moderately high flame.

Then, sear the sausage until well browned on all sides; add in the remaining ingredients and stir to combine.

Allow it to simmer over low heat for 10 minutes or until thickened slightly.

Nutrition:

Calories 381 kcal | Fat: 18g | Carbs: 9.8g | Protein: 25g.

62. Low Carb Avocado Toasts with Homemade Seed Crackers and 3 toppings

Prep Time:	Cooking Time:	Servings:
20 min	45 min	3

Ingredient:

Keto Seed Crackers:

- 1½ tbsp. almond flour
- 1½ tbsp. unsalted sunflower seeds
- 1½ tbsp. unsalted pumpkin seeds
- 1½ tbsp. flaxseed or chia seeds
- 1½ tbsp. sesame seeds
- ½ tbsp. ground psyllium husk powder
- ½ tsp. salt
- 1¼ tbsp. melted coconut oil
- ½ cup. boiling water.

Toppings:

- 3 ripe avocados
- 3 lime (or lemon)
- Black ground pepper, to taste
- Sea salt, to taste
- Fresh chili pepper, to taste
- 3 softly boiled or poached eggs
- 3 handfuls Romaine lettuce
- 3 pinches of parsley
- 6 fin slices of smoked (wild) salmon
- 3 handfuls mixed lettuce
- 3 pinches of dill.

Direction:

Keto Seed Crackers:

Preheat the oven to 300°F.

Mix all dry ingredients in a bowl. Add boiling water and oil. Mix together well.

Keep working the dough until it forms a ball and has a gel-like consistency.

Place the dough on a baking sheet lined with parchment paper.

Add another paper on top and use a rolling pin to flatten the dough evenly.

Remove the upper paper and bake on the lower rack for about 40-45 minutes, check occasionally. Seeds are heat sensitive so pay close attention towards the end.

Turn off the oven and leave the crackers to dry in the oven.

Once dried and cool, break into 9 equal pieces and spread a generous amount of butter on top.

Avocado Toasts:

Slice avocados lengthwise.

Remove the seeds and the skin.

Mash or slice avocados.

Season with lime or lemon juice, black pepper and sea salt.

Top all the seed crackers with avocado.

Topping 1: top 3 crackers with finely sliced chili pepper (seeds removed).

Topping 2: top other 3 crackers with a softly boiled or poached eggs, finely chopped parsley and shredded Romaine lettuce.

Topping 3: top last 3 crackers with smoked salmon, dill and mixed young lettuce leaves.

Enjoy!

Nutrition:

Calories 572 kcal | Fat: 46.5g | Carbs: 5.7g | Protein: 26.1g.

63. Tortilla Breakfast Casserole

Prep Time:	Cooking Time:	Servings:
8 min	45 min	12

Ingredients

- 1 lb. bacon, cooked and crumbled
- 1 lb. pork sausage, cooked and crumbled
- 1 lb. package diced ham
- 10 8-inch tortillas, cut in half
- 8 large eggs
- 1½ cups milk
- ½ tsp. salt
- ½ tsp. pepper
- ½ tsp. garlic powder
- ½ tsp. hot sauce
- 2 cups shredded Cheddar cheese
- 1 cup Mozzarella or Monterrey Jack cheese
- 2 tsp. butter (or nonstick spray oil).

Direction

Spread 2 teaspoons of butter on a 9x13-inch baking dish or sprinkle it with nonstick spray oil.

Bake ⅓ layer of tortillas in the bottom of the pot and cover with baked bacon and ⅓ layer of cheese.

Place another third of the tortillas in the pan and cover with the cooked and chopped sausages.

Then place another third of the cheese in layers.

Repeat with the last tortilla, ham and cheese ⅓.

In a big bowl, blend eggs, milk, salt, pepper, garlic powder, and hot sauce.

Pour the egg mixture evenly over the pot.

If desired, cover overnight and refrigerate or bake immediately.

When you are ready to bake, preheat the oven to 350°F.

Bake covered with foil for 45 minutes.

Open and cook for another 20 minutes until the cheese is completely melted and cooked in a pan.

Nutrition

Calories 447 kcal | Fat: 32.6 g | Carbs: 14.6 g | Protein: 28.6g.

Conclusion

People looking for a quick and effective way to shed excess weight, get high blood sugar levels under control, reduce overall inflammation, and improve physical and mental energy will do their best by following a ketogenic diet plan. But there are special considerations people must take into account when they are beginning the keto diet.

A Ketogenic Diet is something that you should be starting with today for a better lifestyle. The keto diet can help in controlling your body weight and also improve your physical well-being. Not sure from where or how to start with keto?

The keto diet is naturally lower in calories if you follow the recommended levels of food intake. It is not necessary to try to restrict your intake of calories even further. All you need to do is only to eat until you are full and not one bite more. Besides losing weight, the keto diet aims to retrain your body on how to work properly. You will need to learn to trust your body and the signals it sends out to readjust to a proper way of eating.

Do not give up now as there will be quite a few days where you may think to yourself, "Why am I doing this?" and to answer that, focus on the goals you wish to achieve.

Whether you want to stay active, lose weight, look and feel better, or any of that, keto is your solution and a way of life that will ensure you get all you need.

CPSIA information can be obtained
at www.ICGtesting.com
Printed in the USA
BVHW051546090321
602118BV00003B/200